ENDANGERED PATRIOTISM

How We Can Stop the Evil, Hateful, Godless Left from Dividing Our Country

J.W. Tucker III

ISBN: 9798667467076

DEDICATION

To my wife, who is the light of my life, my children, Our Founding Fathers, this book is for you.

CONTENTS

	ACKNOWLEDGMENTS	i
	INTRODUCTION	3
1	THE FLAG	6
2	EDUCATION	14
3	WEALTH AND TAXES	25
4	THE FIRST AMENDMENT	36
5	RELIGIOUS FREEDOM	46
6	ABORTION	54
7	THE SECOND AMENDMENT	60
8	RACE RELATIONS	70
9	IMMIGRATION	82
10	VOTING AND THE ELECTORAL COLLEGE	86
11	STAYING INFORMED	92

ACKNOWLEDGMENTS

I have a few people to thank for the completion of this book. First and foremost, thank you to my wife, who put up with my long hours and provided me countless coffee refills while I researched and wrote.

Thanks to my oldest son, for helping me on the technical side of things, showing me how to use the social media and assisting me in getting this formatted to publish.

I also want to thank the heroes in Conservative Media who help push back against the lies and the manipulation of those on the left and in the mainstream media in hopes of preserving the greatness of Our Nation.

INTRODUCTION

My name is J.W. Tucker III. You, dear reader, may call my "Gunner." It's the name I've gone by among friends and family since I was 14 years old.

I worked for years in the automotive industry. I know firsthand that the American Dream exists and that if we fend off socialists, liberals, big government, and endless regulation it can exists for each and every American that commits himself to hard work and personal responsibility.

I'm a restless spirit with a thirst for knowledge. I spent the early years of my retirement as a substitute teacher, hoping to scratch both itches. I was aghast by the state of our education system and when I refused to conform to godless, feminist, reverse-racist, "scientific" curriculum it resulted in the end of my brief foray into substitute teaching.

I guess I had known about the extent and depravity of the liberal agenda, but it took firsthand experience with this godless, America-hating machine to fully realize the scope of their plans and the effects of their carnage. They won't stop until America as we know it is dead and our citizens spit in the face of the One, True God. I made it my crusade from that day forward to stay informed and educate my fellow citizenry. My weapon of choice in this endeavor has been my computer and keyboard.

I began by sending out newsletters to my friends and family on the AOL. I did this for years. Occasionally, my thoughts would make the rounds on the Facebook. Or so I am told - I don't do the social media.

I'm like our president: a self-made man. I am my own researcher, writer, and editor. I tried to submit some of my work to a local publisher, but some of their editing suggestions made it a non-starter. First of all, if it's important to me then it's a proper noun. I'm a Christian and I'm an American. But I'm also a Patriot who loves God, the Constitution, our Nation, our Soldiers, and our Rights! If my decision to capitalize those words or, better yet, my decision NOT to capitalize godless leftism offends you then, well, feel free to gift this book to someone who isn't offended by love for our Great Country.

I can't wait for you to dig into this book. It's a quick read in content and form, but it contains ideas that I firmly believe are indispensable to the survival of our Country. This is the Greatest Nation on Earth. Let's keep it that way.

CHAPTER ONE: THE FLAG

I pledge allegiance to THE FLAG of the United States of America, and to the Republic for which it stands, one nation UNDER GOD, indivisible, with liberty and justice for all.

I'm going to say something right now that hopefully you, dear reader, is brave enough to admit, but it is something that the liberal elites who control our bureaucracy and the mainstream media don't have the guts to say: The USA is the greatest country in the entire world. It's right there in the pledge. One nation *under God*. Not two nations. Not one nation under Allah or one nation under some gender-confused, skinny-jeans wearing sissy.

We are blessed to live in a time where not only do we know that Jesus Christ is our Lord and Savior, but that the United States of America is a holy country - as long as the godless liberals don't have their way. God gave us the Bible, the greatest book ever written. It's infallible and divinely inspired. Similarly, He divinely inspired our Founding Fathers to declare our independence, develop and ratify the Constitution, and solidify our standing as the greatest country to ever grace this magnificent planet.

Now, sit there and think about that. Let it sink in. If God divinely inspired our Founders to develop the greatest country in the world, the greatest thing since the Bible, do you think that He, in His infinite wisdom and limitless power, would allow us to develop a lame flag? Of course not.

Now, as obvious as this is to patriots, I need to spell it out a little more clearly for our liberal friends: If God gave us the Bible, gave us the greatest country ever in similar fashion,

AND made darned sure that this country had the coolest flag ever, do you really think that he'd want a bunch of football-playing thugs disrespecting it? Exactly.

Colin Kaepernick - yeah, that's right, if any of you liberal snowflakes are reading this, we don't need trigger warnings even though any self-respecting patriot should vomit in their mouth at the sight of that animal's name - is a lost soul. Even still, I pray for him every single day. It's true. You should too. You should never delight in the hell-bound path of one of your enemies. Don't give in, don't compromise (you can't compromise with evil, which is what the liberals don't understand), but pray that he will see the light, repent, and square himself with the One True God, His Son, His Country, and His Flag.

But, until that day comes, Kaepernick is an agent of evil, spitting in the face of God and dividing our country. Mr. Quarterback sits there in his ivory tower, counting his millions, millions he made playing a *game* in a country whose freedoms and luxuries he has always enjoyed but for which he's never sacrificed. I've tried to wrap my head around his "logic," but it's impossible. Like trying to make 2 + 2 = 5 add up.

Kaepernick says he wants to protest against systemic oppression against people of color. First off, on more than one occasion I've been asked to leave an establishment for using the term "coloreds," yet Mr. Too-Good-to-Stand can say "color" 'til the cows come home. I'm sorry, but I have a hard time getting lectured about race relations from someone who has made millions forcing his evil views on me while, at the same time, I've had my first amendment rights trampled on at multiple eateries and been told that I, a white man, am not allowed to use words that are spoken freely by men of *color*. In my experience racism is alive and well, by golly, but it sure as heck not what Kaepernick and his sycophants in the lamestream media think it is.

The real problem is reverse racism. White men have been held down for too long. We've got a warrior in the White House right now doing everything he can to keep things fair and equal for every American, but minority activists and feminists are fighting dirty. Sound far-fetched? Maybe, until you realize that the Democrat Party's last two nominees for president were a Muslim, non-white "American" and a closeted lesbian.

Yet, despite the fact that I've established this anti-men, anti-white agenda, do you see folks like me dishonoring our Flag? *Hell no.* Because we're not a bunch of snowflakes that throw hissy-fits and act out when things go our way. We man up. We're not a bunch of Colin Kaepernicks.

That's why I made sure to burn every last stitch of Nike apparel I owned. When that evil company had the audacity to give Kaepernick more money, fame, and influence for his godless agenda, I had to take a stand. Luckily for me, it didn't take long. I didn't own a ton of stuff. For starters, I'm a Member's Mark man, and the Sam's Club doesn't usually carry Nike. But I'm also a husband and father, and I feel a greater sense of responsibility to my wife and kids than I do the manager at Footlocker when the next Air Jordans come out.

That said, I did own a few items, a couple of pairs of sneakers, some T-shirts, and a hoodie. They made great kindling. A few buddies and I made an evening out of it, creating a bonfire and enjoying fellowship. Because that's how you get things done, not by throwing a tantrum and acting out but by joining up with real Americans and supporting a good cause.

Unfortunately, so much of our country is drifting aimlessly and supporting such evil attacks on our God and our Nation. While I was researching and writing this book, the NFL had the audacity to apologize to Colin Kapernick! This was a league led by owners who I believed were led by good, honest, decent job creators and they sent their puppet Roger Goodell out to pander to the Black Lives Matter thugs and, essentially, defecate on our Flag

Well, I'll tell you, I'm a private individual. I don't really trust the Internet but my better half did make us a Facebook account to keep up with pictures of our grandbabies. I try to stay off the social media, but you can best believe that I got on the computer and sent a loud and clear message to the NFL. It was the same message I sent them each and every Sunday when I tuned in to see Kaepernick insulting our Flag and our Soldiers: You've just lost yourself a longtime fan!

Some will argue that it's dramatic, but I don't care. I'm not politically correct. I'm not woke. I'm a red-blooded, God-fearing American Patriot, and I love that Flag and everything for which it stands. When I wake up each morning, walk outside to grab the paper, and stop to salute our Flag and recite the pledge, I don't get misty-eyed because of the beauty of the words (although they're magnificent). I think about my family's proud history of fighting for our right to live free - despite the left's best efforts to stifle my views and opinions.

'It's just a flag,' they'll tell you, hoping to wear down the resolve of your patriotism. That's globalist nonsense. The flag is more than a few fibers stitched together. It's the representation of the greatest Nation that God bestowed upon this planet, and it embodies a Patriotic worldview that not only instills me and countless other Patriots with a sense of pride, but sets the foundation for this book and the views it contains. I will not apologize for loving my Country, my God, or my Flag. When you finish this book, I bet you'll feel the same way.

CHAPTER TWO: EDUCATION

I'm structuring this book simply. There are a handful of topics that I believe represent the most important struggles facing our country. We are literally fighting off evil on the left as we battle for the soul of our Nation. While I hesitate to place such a premium on education - after all, it's the stepping stone toward liberal colleges and anti-American academia - it's the breeding ground for the evil secularist agenda that is indoctrinating our children.

The biggest problem facing the education system in this country is the fact that liberals have removed the greatest teacher to ever exist from the equation: Jesus Christ. Why on earth would you establish an institution of learning and not have our Lord and Savior as the foundation? I know it's because our education officials are evil and godless, but I mean it to be rhetorical as much as anything.

When I was a child, we could pray in school. Today? Not so much. After I retired, I stayed busy by working as a substitute teacher. *Stayed*, past tense, being the operative word. I led my homeroom in prayer each morning that I worked, the principal delivered an ultimatum telling me to stop, and I refused to have my religious freedoms stifled in such a manner so I gave up substitute teaching.

When I think back on the experience, it really drives home just how messed up our education system has become. I have developed a fool-proof system to revitalize our schools and lay the groundwork for a return to the America that you, I, and all other Patriots love.

Bring Back Prayer

This is a biggie. It's no wonder that nutjobs are shooting up schools when they start each morning without giving thanks to the Good Lord. Even if they come from troubled, godless homes, that sprinkling of prayer each morning provides enough grace to keep our children saved.

I grew up in the 1950s. Boys dressed like boys, girls dressed like girls, and our teachers were men and women of faith *and* they didn't have to hide it. We prayed every day. Want to know how many of my classmates were killed by an assault rifle? Zero. Guns don't kill people, crazy people whose lives have been ruined by godless liberals kill people.

And when I say prayer, I mean *real* prayer. I don't mean getting on your knees and facing Mecca. You might as well start praying to Satan. I mean closing your eyes, bowing your head, and praying in the name of Jesus Christ.

Let the Bible Set the Curriculum

I'll never understand the liberal rationale on anything, but especially the Bible. God gave us an unimpeachably perfect book that provides an answer to literally any of life's questions. Why on earth are we not utilizing this resource in our schools?

When I was subbing, it got to the point that they wouldn't let me near the science classes because I wouldn't teach the filth they asked of me. I mean, GOD said that the heavens and the earth were created in six days. A man named Darwin has a THEORY of evolution that implies that it took much longer to create. I guess maybe if I was under the impression that I evolved from a monkey that THEORY might make sense, but since I KNOW that GOD made everything with a snap of HIS fingers I don't need to entertain such foolishness.

We need to spend less time on the Big Bang Theory and more time on the early books of The Bible. When you tell kids that the earth and the universe are a bazillion gajillion years old, everything seems insignificant, so they don't question you when you start navel-gazing about outer space, cellular structure, and whatever irrelevant nonsense that liberal scientists make up as they go along as they try to come up with new explanations that discredit God. When students realize that everything was created roughly 6,000 years ago it makes it much easier to focus on other subjects.

Remove Liberal Bias

When you expose modern-day "science" for the convoluted witchcraft that it really is, you still have some work today to de-secularize the education.

You've got to be careful with biology. Kids are on the Internet all the time now, so they are being indoctrinated in more places than just the classroom. On days I feel discouraged I feel like we've lost the battle against the homosexual agenda. Deep down, I know we can turn that around, but I let that sense of defeat strengthen my resolve against the He-Shes and their Transgender Agenda.

When you bring God back into the equation, you can educate our youngsters about sexuality in a healthy way. Teenagers are filled with hormones, fact. They have urges, fact. But if boys don't think about girls and vice versa then they should be sent away for intensive therapy, fact. The moment we opened the door of an abomination like homosexuality being natural rather than a lifestyle choice, we kicked God out and invited Satan in.

But Mr. Gunner, one of my students once asked me (I told them Mr. Tucker was my dad and asked for them to call me Mr. Gunner), aren't there examples of homosexuality in other species? You think Satan can't make a dolphin gay? I shot back. Checkmate.

If we don't start hitting back on the fundamentals of sexuality, pretty soon they're going to be forbidding out kids to identify with their birth gender and force them to use the opposite bathroom.

Re-Establish Gender Roles

Boys belong in P.E., girls belong in Home-Ec. Look, I'm sorry, it has to be said. I'm not a total fuddy-duddy. If there is time in the schedule to let the girls run some laps or slap a volleyball around I don't mind. They need their exercise too.

But once we eradicate the secular filth from science class, we need to return to the more traditional forms of education that prepared young men and women for the societal roles for which they're best suited. My wife is a phenomenal cook. Her ninth grade Home-Ec teacher instilled in her a lifelong love of culinary pursuits. Do you think I would get such tasty meals if her guidance counselor made that class optional and encouraged her to consider other electives as an alternative? Further, do you think she would have been well equipped to stay home and raise our three beautiful children? Exactly.

Once you return to the one, true science book that the Good Lord gave us *and* you stop confusing our children by letting girls take boy classes and boys take girl classes, you'll see that things will finally start taking shape.

Cut the Cutesy Revisionist History

The history books that I used in the 1950s were perfect. Sure, they need to be updated to cover the span of time between then and now, to include such things as Reagan's destruction of Communism, the liberation of Iraq, the Tea Party and Make America Great Again movements, and other Patriotic conquests. But for all intents and purposes, the history I learned should be the history my children learn.

I don't need some punk gender studies or African American studies major to tell me that my history has been white-washed. White men broke bread with the Indians and spread a superior way of life across America, planting the seeds for the greatest Nation on earth. You want to tell me those ends don't justify the means? And consider the alternative, that Indians were helpless to stop the spread of White settlers. If I made that argument, I would get called a racist White supremacist.

It's the same with slavery. Black people want to hold me responsible for things that happened before I was born. But if they hold a grudge against me because other white people owned slaves centuries ago, why don't they hold grudges against their fellow blacks who sold one another to the slaves back in Africa? Of course, the Black Lives Matter thugs don't care about black-on-black crime so why should care that, when you really think about it, that black people are responsible for slavery. I hate slavery, and you should too, but I don't hold it against black folks that their ancestors sold their fellow man out to slave traders.

That's the risk you run when you try to fix what ain't broken vis a vis our history books. In many ways, ignorance is bliss. Why try to make Indians or black people feel weak or flawed when we can instead focus on the fruits of the American colonists: The United States of America.

Ditch the Computers

I never minded that my kids fiddled with the Atari or the Nintendo - in moderation. But you can't tell me that the wussification of our country hasn't been hastened in some measure by the proliferation of computers. Some people complain that we're taking the focus off handwriting, but I don't stop there. I think we should ditch computers altogether.

When you tether a child to a computer screen, you increase his likelihood of shying away from masculine interests like hunting, playing sports, or talking to girls. On top of that, you're spending more time teaching kids to type than developing their handwriting. Not only is that creating a Big Brother scenario where we are removing an element of uniqueness from each person, sending us further down the road of a dystopian society, but we're conditioning our boys to behave like secretaries. More gender and sexual confusion.

When you lose the computers the students fall into their roles. They become more well-rounded individuals. They also have more time to learn because their substitute teacher doesn't have to spend half the class learning how to operate the projector because their normal teacher left a computer presentation.

CHAPTER THREE: WEALTH AND TAXES

Liberals hate our country. You need look no further than their bitter resentment of capitalism. They hate hard-working Patriots who are able to fulfill the American Dream. They want nothing more than to create a socialist "paradise" where God is shut out, hoodlums run our cities, and the brave men and women of the Heartland can't fulfill their God-given right to work hard and advance their station in life.

Consider President Donald Trump. This is an America-loving, Gun-supporting, God-fearing, Bible-believing BILLIONAIRE who selflessly put his wealthy lifestyle on hold to roll up his sleeves and help get America back on track after eight years of leading from behind. Liberals love weaklings, that's why they worship at the altar of Barack Hussein "Apology Tour" Obama.

Because Donald Trump is a successful White man, the left demands that he just apologize for his very existence. *I'm sorry I'm a White male who loves my country, dared to work hard, and built a billion-dollar Christian enterprise.* Obviously you and I know that he has nothing to apologize for, but even if he humored the snowflakes and begged forgiveness for being the Ultimate Male they would still find new ways to denigrate and mock this great man.

It boggles the mind that President Trump has faced so much resistance. It boggles it even more when you consider everything this man has been able to accomplish despite historic opposition from the Democrats. But the godless heathens like Alexandria Occasio Cortez and her "squad" hate success, hate men, hate our country, and hate our economic system, so what do you expect?

But though they do their best to distract our country with cute little diagrams on C-SPAN and snarky Tweets on the Twitter, they know that deep down the silent majority of patriotic men and women loathe everything they stand for. So they have to lie and cheat to get ahead, hoping their band of beltway insiders can stack the deck against the *real* America. Donald Trump is the perfect microcosm of our country and our economic system, and that's why people become so unhinged with Trump Derangement Syndrome.

President Trump's is a classic tale of a Christian Patriot pulling himself up by the bootstraps and fulfilling the American Dream. The Trump Organization came from basically *nothing*. Oh, hey liberals, don't believe me? Take it from the man himself:

"My whole life, really has been a no," President Donald J. Trump told a group of supporters during the 2016 campaign. "It has not been easy for me," he added, noting that the only thing that counted as a leg up was a "small loan" of a million dollars.

Liberals freaked out about the "million dollars" bit, going back to the well of Gotcha Journalism that tarnished the reputation of Sarah Palin in 2008. Now, a million dollars might be a lot to a bunch of Millennials that only leave Mommy and Daddy's house to go blog at Starbuck's, but let's put that into perspective. Donald Trump is worth about $4 billion. Do you know how little $1 million is in comparison? It is .00025% of his net worth. ARE YOU KIDDING ME? That's a drop in the bucket.

Want to see a comparison that shows just how out of touch those liberals are? If you work 40 hours a week flipping burgers, you'd earn a little over $15,000 each year. You know what .00025% of $15,000 is? $3.77, or, not even the cost of a slice of avocado toast.

So yes, liberals, you're right, Donald Trump has been so pampered. Based on his net worth he was given what amounted to the cost of one Big Mac. Do you think you could take Big Mac money and make it into a BILLION dollars? This is America so, of course, you *could* in theory, but it takes a special kind of person to make it happen. That's Donald J. Trump.

I know liberals are wanting to change how we do math, but even a common core student could see that when you can turn the price of a McDonald's value meal into a billion dollars we don't have a wealth distribution problem, we have a 'I don't want to work, can you just hand me money please?' problem. I get so sick and tired of godless liberals going on TV or the Internet and vilifying our richest men and women, as if they aren't the reason has the opportunity to get up each morning and go earn a living. Consider my story.

I was once one of those burger flippers and I put myself through college doing it. No debt, and I even had money left over to maintain my own car and take the future Mrs. Tucker out each morning. I was able to find a job right out of college, but I'm grateful for my employment in the fast-food industry. I worked hard and was appreciative. *That* is the problem with today's youth. When Mrs.

Tucker and I go out for Sunday lunch after church you'd be amazed at the lack of dedication we see. It's frustrating: young men and women on phones, looking tired or hungover, and sometimes putting out the vibe that they don't want to be there. Why on earth would McDonald's, Wendy's, or anyone want to pay these people are respectable wage when they don't respect themselves or their job?

I'm living proof that you can go to college without debt and start a family with one of these jobs. If these young people had an ounce of discipline and respect they could make it happen for themselves too. Of course, that's not likely to happen any time soon considering they aren't in church on Sunday mornings.

You won't hear the liberal elites speak so bravely though. They would rather vilify the job creators than be honest with people whose jobs they subsidize. I made the mistake of scrolling beyond our grandbabies' pictures on Facebook at one point during the Covid-19 "crisis," and encountered a post about our country's concentration of wealth and how the "rich got richer" during the pandemic. It made my blood boil.

The wealth of all of our country's billionaires grew by almost $650 billion during the crisis. Obviously, that's great news. Our job creators and providers are able to stand on surer ground, a strong signal that our economy is humming right along under President Trump. However, the misguided young lady who shared this post was complaining.

I clicked on this girl's profile, and not only is she whining about our hardworking billionaires rolling up their sleeves during an economic crisis and making lemonade out of lemons, but apparently she is a teacher (I shudder for the youth of her school district) who wanted to forgo in-person learning until the "crisis" was over. I sent her a message, and while I never heard back I think it best sums up the wealth-inequality "problem" in our country.

Dear (name withheld),

I came across your commentary about the continued success of our country's most successful men and women. I took the liberty of perusing your profile and discovered that you are a teacher. I would hope that a woman who dedicates her life to furthering education could educate herself on how our economy works.

These men and women, including our Great President Donald Trump, whom you seem to have an agenda against, have been able to work hard during this pandemic when many people, including you and many other teachers, complain that society expects them to work. You can't have it both ways. If you want to over-react about a case of sniffles that's your prerogative. But you probably shouldn't be a teacher and you definitely shouldn't be paid during your self-imposed exile, much less complain about job creators who have braved this uncertain time, worked hard, and continued their unprecedented success. They are model Americans, Patriots that you and I should strive to emulate. They shouldn't be mocked or ridiculed for being successful, especially when they are so kind to share their success with the working-class men and women who make our country go.

I hope you'll take this message in the spirit in which it was intended, reflect on my words, and come through with a clearer understanding for that which all Americans should inspire.

Warmest regards,
J.W. Tucker III

I do my best not to get angry with the younger generation. To paraphrase a quote that is often attributed to Winston Churchill, but whose true authorship is unknown, to be young and not be liberal is to have no heart, to be old and not be conservative is to have no brain. But, when these old, brainless liberals seek to destroy our country, compassionate understanding is a little harder to convey.

Our wealthiest Americans still share what they have and help our country's men and women to provide and, if they work hard, climb the ladder of the American Dream even though, increasingly, people want to spit in the face of their hard work and accomplishment. Not only do these punks and thugs want to "feel the Bern" and get paid for doing nothing, and not only do they want to complain about their compensation at jobs for which they bring no dedication and respect, but they have the audacity to ask for all of this *and* demand that the wealthiest folks, who are already prohibitively taxed after decades of socialism masquerading as Democrat Party policies, actually pay more in taxes!

I'll give Bernie Sanders credit for one thing, he probably helped us stop Hillary Clinton from becoming president. Obviously, President Trump could have beaten Miss Benghazi with one hand tied behind his back if it was a fair fight, but considering that the Obama administration and the Russians were conspiring against him it was all he could do to fend her off. Bernie getting his supporters lathered up with promises of 'free money and unicorns for all' meant she had to fend off attacks from the even farther left (which seems impossible, but is somehow true).

But Bernie deserves the same amount of credit as a broken clock being right twice a day. He may have helped stymie Hillary, but he got the misguided souls of our country even more fired up about turning away from God, hard work, and the principles that turned our country into the Greatest Nation on Earth. The Democrat Party may have conspired against him *twice* to avoid the nomination, but his carnage has been wrought. He has given free-loaders, atheists, and socialists an emblem to unite under. He has also strengthened their resolve.

Our country as we know it is under attack by godless socialists. Luckily, we can preserve our economic system, fair taxation, and job creation by remaining true to our principles. So, you Patriots, work hard, respect yourselves, and vote.

CHAPTER FOUR: THE FIRST AMENDMENT

Yes, Dear Patriots, at the time of this book's writing the First Amendment still exists. Barely. It may be hanging by a thread thanks to America-hating leftists who want nothing more than to see our proud Nation go under in favor of some globalist utopia, but as long as we speak up and defend it it will never fail.

There has never been a more perfect example of the modern liberal's assault on our God-given right to Free Speech than the nonsense that has transpired during the Covid-19 "crisis." It shows the godless synergy of our enemy's on the left. The mainstream media hyped up cases of the sniffles, falsely attributed other unrelated deaths to the coronavirus, and whipped the weak-minded among us into a tizzy. This set the table for the shadow government of liberal elites to impose fascist policies, hoping to use a hoax "pandemic" to steal overnight the rights they have spent decades undermining.

I had a buddy, a proud Patriot and Christian, who passed on to the next life early during the pandemic. He died of a heart attack, but his wife told me that the hospital asked questions about respiratory issues and, when she wasn't paying attention, established the cause of death as Covid-19. I read about stories all the time on the Internet about these things happening all over the country. A young man choking on his hamburger at a Memorial Day gathering died of Covid-19. An elderly couple killed in a car accident - Covid-19. A young child killed by a gator in Florida - Covid-19.

After months of padding the numbers by marking every death under the sun as the result of Covid-19 it was time for the leftists to let their liberal flag fly. They lied about the severity of the sickness, used the media to scare our citizenry, and then capitalized on that fear to steal our rights and institute fascist policies. Sadly, many of you reading this have been victimized by this assault on our inalienable rights. As I write this, over 25 states - HALF OF OUR COUNTRY - is being subjected to unconstitutional executive orders mandating the use of facemasks.

Forget for a moment that the "science" behind the masks doesn't compute. If I have a minor case of Covid-19 then what good is it going to do if I breathe and breathe into my mask and let those germs collect and grow? It's just common sense that masks do not work.

But even if they did, it is my right as a Free-Thinking American to not wear the darned things. I'm sorry, I'm not going to let the Gestapo take away my rights because you're afraid I might give you the case of the sniffles. I'll touch on it more in my chapter on guns, but it reminds me of those overly dramatic parents that think a handful of gun tragedies should result in taking away my Constitutionally guaranteed right to unfettered access to firearms.

I'm a big fan of Buck Sexton, the former CIA analyst who now counters the lies and fake news of the mainstream media on his podcast. I came across one of his posts on the Twitter about the issue and it is absolutely spot on. "Still wondering where in the Constitution it says that all your freedoms can be suspended on capricious whim of a state governor for as long as he wants because of a disease that has a 99.7% survival rate," he wrote. AMEN.

When do we, as law-abiding citizens of the Greatest Nation on Earth get OUR Me Too movement? I don't doubt that legitimate rape happens and in those instances my heart goes out to the young ladies who were subjected to such awful sexual encounters. But, telling me I have to wear a mask when I want to go to the grocery store is far more egregious of a violation of my rights than a promiscuous young lady who has a little too much to drink at a party, the next morning regrets her decision to get into a one-time romantic involvement, and decides that she was raped and now shelters herself from "triggers" (even though she continues to dress immodestly after the fact).

These governors and mayors, godless leftists all of them, are literally raping the Proud Citizens of this Great Nation. As I write this, even some of my favorite business are kowtowing to the pressure from leftists, the media, and the government to strip us of our rights. For the first few months that this all went down I still had the pleasure of shopping at Wal-Mart. That stopped on July 20, 2020 when they decided that aiding and abetting the destruction of Our Constitution was more important than my continued patronage. Mrs. Tucker and I will take our busy elsewhere from now on, thank you very much.

But before Wal-Mart turned into a Nazi ghetto, shopping there for my groceries gave me plenty of opportunity to commend fellow Patriots while warning misguided souls. I frequently came across Patriotic Mothers who had two, three, sometimes even four or more children with them. Those amazing ladies weren't going to wear masks nor were they going to let a left-wing hoax make them keep their kids at home. I'd make a point to shake all of their hands, pat them on the back, and occasionally give them a kiss on the cheek. Their dedication to the ideals of our country would bring tears to my eye.

On the other hand, there were plenty of fools who provided me teachable moments against liberal nonsense. "You do realize you're helping the left-wing media steal your rights and putting yourself at a higher risk of getting sick, right?" I'd often ask. I resisted the urge to insult, even though the facemask has became a symbol of the smug sense of leftist superiority. Deep down, I love all of my fellow Countrymen, even those who are lost. Jesus cared more about the lost sheep and that is my example. I hate leftism, but I don't hate leftists. I'm hoping they can get right with their God and their Country before it's too late.

Most of these folks remained misguided. Mostly, they ignored me. Some mustered the occasional nonsensical stammer in reply. But there were same who would take me on, not realizing that they were engaging with, and I hate to come across as boastful, a bit of an expert in the art of debate.

I'm just looking out for you, you people without masks are putting us at greater risk, sir. That was a solid example of the responses I would get. Add in a few expletives for the younger, thuggier folks who would respond to me.

I would roll my eyes, calmly explain that they were betraying their Country, falling for leftist pseudo-science, and, more or less, helping to turn the United States of America into Nazi Germany 2.0. Few would engage beyond that. I like to think that as those folks stormed off with their shopping carts that at least some of them let my logic sink in, removed their masks, and joined you, me, and the other Patriots in standing against oppression and tyranny.

I'm a reasonable person. We still frequent restaurants even though all of them in our area, to this point, require face-coverings for their staff. It's required by an unconstitutional executive order, but I recognize that these restaurants, often small businesses, are stuck between a rock and a hard place.

But there are a few establishments who we will never darken their doorstep again. It's a shame. My old pharmacy, a locally owned establishment which I liked to use in the name of supporting small businesses, put up a sign that was light on the First Amendment and heavy on the snark, suggesting that if I had a problem with their mask policy that there were other pharmacies in the area. Fair enough. If they don't want my business because I value my rights then so be it. I did have to pop in for one last visit to let them know that I would never support an unconstitutional business and I would make sure to let all of my friends, family, and readers know about their "values."

These are the slippery slope politics that the left has been practicing for decades and now the chickens have come home to roost. If I don't want to wear a seatbelt that's my prerogative. If I have a few beers at a cookout but deem myself sober enough to drive, that's my prerogative - I think I know my alcohol tolerance a little bit better than Big Brother. I'm not the type that gallavants around with shirts, pants, or shoes, but every time I see one of those ridiculous signs on the entrance to a store, I roll my eyes and shudder for what has happened to this great country.

I am a Christian. I am an American. I'm a White Male. I'm Conservative. I'm proud of ALL of these things, and I won't apologize for them. If I want to do something or not do something, if I want to be somewhere then that is the right guaranteed to be my Creator and my Founding Fathers.

Leftists will attack you for feeling this way. They love being told what to do and being restricted (unless they want to fornicate or have an abortion). Because they are followers, they are sheep, and then need Big Government to tell them how to run their life. Their lack of intelligence and integrity makes them yearn to be led around like pigs to a slaughter, but over here in the Free World we Patriots yearn for Life, Liberty, and the Pursuit of Happiness.

CHAPTER FIVE: RELIGIOUS FREEDOM

Our Founding Fathers were divinely inspired men of God. Christians who established a country that held freedom from religious persecution as one of its primary tenets. That's a fact. Sorry, liberals.

For decades, Christian Patriots lived in peace and freedom. However, for most of my life, my Lord and Savior, and, by proxy, my Country, has been under attack by the godless left. They have sought to persecute Christianity at every turn. They are doing Satan's work, but I think we know how things will shake out between God and Satan.

Nevertheless, it is our job to call it out and fight against it.

I touched on it in the chapter about education, but the left and the ACLU (Lucifer's law firm, if ever there was one) have left our schools and our children for dead. Every time I read about school shootings I shake my head. My heart weeps for the children and the families, but what do you expect when you remove God from the equation?

Now, invariably, those lefties will try to single out Our One True God and pretend to have faith in false gods in order to tear down Jesus Christ. Oh, it's not fair to the Jews and the Muslims in these schools. Really? Can they not read the Bible? I get called a racist and a bigot constantly by people who are too ignorant to realize that I have nothing against Jews and Middle-Easterners - so long as they repent of their sins, rebuke their blasphemous religions, and embrace Jesus Christ as their Savior. I'm not sure why this logic eludes the minions on the left, but it's a battle I will continue to fight all the same.

You see, their love of Jews and Muslims comes from the place of their hatred for Our Country and Our God. First off, Muslims hate America just about as much as liberals do. (Remind me how many of those hijackers on 9/11 were Christian, will you?) So they support radical Muslim terrorists and their right to praise Allah not because they respect the idea of religion, but because they can kill two birds with one stone: undermine Christianity and promote groups that hate America.

The crazy thing? I don't hate them either. I hate what they stand for, but I still pray for them. Just as Jews and Muslims have every right in the world to crack open the Bible, learn the Truth, and repent of their wicked ways, so too do purple-haired lesbians who get angry when you use gendered pronouns.

But just because I pray for them doesn't mean that I become complacent in my zest to defeat their evil, godless ideology. Compromise, when it comes to matters of Good and evil is wrong. Liberals will try to suck you into their vortex of compromise and participation ribbons, so you have to be careful to stand your ground.

Take the homosexuals. They have spent decades normalizing the homosexual agenda, quite successfully I might add. But because you, me, and countless other Christian Patriots rigidly cling to the Truth, their half-measures seeking to make the unacceptable acceptable have failed. First, they made sodomy illegal. I don't think I need to remind you of how God deals with sodomites, but it isn't pretty. Then they got civil unions, then "marriage." We fought tooth and nail against these assaults on our Christian beliefs, but they were able to succeed in these battles. We must not give up on the war.

Look, I have nothing against gay and lesbian folks. They too can repent, ask God for forgiveness, and accept Jesus Christ as their savior. I'm not a bigot. But, you can't expect me to sit here and condone such unnatural behavior in any way, shape, or form.

But that is exactly what liberals expect. They foist these demonic, godless "marriages" on our society, allow these perverts to adopt our children, and they expect us to make wedding cakes for them with smiles on our faces? I think not.

At the end of the day, it's not natural. Last I checked, our Conservative business owners were still Americans. Why can't they refuse service to a gay couple on the grounds that they are insulting God with their disgusting union? What's next, will the ACLU expect them to bake cakes for weirdos who want to marry dogs? Horses? CHILDREN?

It becomes a circular argument for these people. What makes my religion better than anyone else's? Um, well, if you get the chance to read the Bible you'll find that there is One True God and One True religion. You'll also note that this is a Christian Nation. So, do the math. A perfect book describing a perfect religion that directly led to the founding of a perfect Country. Does this sound like a tomato, tomahto situation to you? Of course not.

I've noticed the new wrinkle that many liberals have added to their quest to destroy our country: co-opting Christianity for their sick, perverted agenda. Every day it seems I read about this "Christian" church letting ladies lead or that "Christian" church marrying the gays. Look, I can put on cowboy boots, a cowboy hat, and a tag that says 'Hi, My Name is John Wayne,' but that doesn't make me John Wayne. The truth of the matter is that most people, even those who claim to be Christian, are going to Hell. It's sad, but it's their own fault.

The Bible lays out a clear foundation for how to live and worship and anyone that deviates deserves the hellfire. I come from a long line of independent thinkers who have applied their love of intellectual pursuits to the Good Book. I'm blessed to know that my father, his father, and his father's father all wrestled with the theology and, of their own volition, found the narrow path to Salvation. I too am a humble servant of Jesus Christ and I am grateful for the knowledge that unlike most of the population that I will be called

Home when I leave this mortal coil. I suspect, dear reader, that you can take comfort in a similar assurance.

Some godless leftists think they can slap a "Christian" veneer onto their heathen lifestyles and behave as if they can lecture Real Christians on matters of Faith. You got Mayor Pete Whatshisname, for instance. If you, I, or any other Patriot went straight from being the mayor of a small city to running for president we might be applauded for our pluck, but we'd be laughed out of the campaign if we were ever acknowledged in the first place. Republicans don't nominate unqualified fools for higher office.

But because Mayor Pete is a homosexual who hides his radical politics behind his "Christian" faith and his "marriage," liberals leapt at the chance to make him famous. They hoped he could fool the Heartland just because he looked like a respectable man who claimed to have Christian faith and unimpeachable military experience. But they couldn't, and the radicals of their party opted for an even more radical candidate who promised to revive Obama-era socialism and oppression.

That doesn't mean that this is the end of Mayor Pete or the politics of hijacking Christianity for nefarious means. That will be the next battle for the soul of our Country and the fight for Religious Freedom. We must insist that our country remain Proud, Free and unapologetically Christian. We can't let America be tainted by impostors, be they false gods or distorted depictions of Our God.

CHAPTER SIX: ABORTION

There is no greater sin on our Nation's history than the legalization and spread of abortion. Take the evils of slavery and the horrors of the Holocaust. Multiply them together. Now double it. That gives you a pretty good idea of how awful this insidious practice is.

That's a pretty controversial take, but when it comes to ripping babies out of their mother's womb and leaving them for dead I don't mince words. There is nothing more evil, and it's a simple fix. Make it illegal to murder babies. That shouldn't be so complicated.

My wife and I drive to the city to pray outside of abortion clinics at least once a month. Occasionally, I'll bring some literature or signs. Invariably I get accosted by baby murderers, their raging feminist friends, or their spineless boyfriends who hold their hand and reassure them as they murder their child.

Will you adopt her baby? Will you pay for her childcare? They shout. I would laugh if it wasn't so serious.

This is what liberals expect you to do. They want you to endorse their bad decisions and their proclivity to fornicate. Among the freebies they expect from hardworking taxpayers like you and me is contraception. Apparently I'm responsible for making sure you don't get pregnant when you jump from bed to bed. Because my Christian Values aren't compatible with spending money on such evil, then I'm now responsible to raise your child or pay for its upbringing?

How about this: Close your legs and get a job! I'm so sick of the entitled mindset of so many of our fellow citizens. They have grown up in a society where it's fashionable to reject God and the rock-solid values of our Country. Instead of taking personal responsibility they want to live in sinful excess, mock us responsible citizens, and then turn around expect us to either bail them out and carry their dead weight even further or we are somehow responsible for their sinful choices. It's outrageous.

It's also all connected. We could eliminate many of these problems if we returned our education system to conservative principles more in keeping with Christian, American values. We need to stop teaching these kids that it's OK to fornicate, which is exactly what teaching about contraception does. Do you really think the vast majority of our teenagers would be having sex if they weren't being taught ways to make it "safe?"

Don't cite me those stats about abortion numbers under Barack Hussein Obama. First, if they dipped it's because they encouraged kids to have "safe sex" and they had a few years of good luck with their contraceptives of choice. But it's not sustainable. When you encourage sexual permissiveness then sexual carelessness isn't far behind. Soon, just a few years into this liberal paradise we will have an abortion boom of students who were taught that premarital sex is OK, had every other area of personal discipline eroded and stopped using protection, and found themselves in a society that normalized the murder of teeny tiny babies.

The only thing that is protecting us from an avalanche of abortions are Conservative Values that desperately fight off self-centered secular interests. Teach kids that abstinence is the only way, which will tamp down the youthful lust for sexual activity, and, at the same time, educate them on how society should operate. This will grow our Silent Majority and, in time, finally put conservatives in control of all three branches of government, make abortion illegal once and for all, and end this divisive argument.

Will that eradicate all abortion? Probably not. Unfortunately, evil will still exist. But it will lessen the number of women who, for one, have unwanted pregnancies and, two, view abortion as an acceptable option. For those evil stragglers who insist on the procedure there will be no government-funded murder clinics.

Many leftists will present this last point as if it's a reason to keep abortion legal. The logic is something else. Essentially, we should let godless, leftist doctors continue to murder sweet, cuddly babies because there is a chance that women could face complications from back-alley abortions. Really? I don't want anyone to die. I hope women who are inclined to feel this way find Jesus and repent. As I've said many times, I hate the sin not the sinner. But if I'm forced to choose a scenario then, yes, I will take my chances with a handful of willful baby murderers dying as a consequence of their sin than the continued genocide of innocent babies.

Preserve the family unit. Take some responsibility. Don't have sex until your married. Boom, the problem is not only solved, but it also eliminates the need for the weak disingenuous rebuttals from the left.

Pay more taxes for social programs for impoverished mothers, consider adopting unwanted children, yada yada yada. How about get a job, have sex after your married, and don't make me responsible for the consequences of your godless consequences?

CHAPTER SEVEN: THE SECOND AMENDMENT

I think I need a trigger warning for any snowflake who reads this chapter, lest they ruin their book by drowning it in liberal tears. I'm not just a Christian and a Patriot, but I'm a proud Gun Owner. All three go hand in hand, and they make up the backbone of this country.

To debate liberals on matters of guns is to wade into a cesspool of flawed logic and sissiness. Leftists have spent years empowering the weaker sex while tricking many of our Nation's "men" into thinking that masculinity is something for which to be ashamed. So, when we wussify so many of our citizens of course they will be afraid of such awesome, powerful machines and wish to question their worth.

Without guns our country wouldn't be here. It's a simple fact whether liberals like it or not. We single-handedly took down what had been, to that point, the greatest empire the world had ever seen. And we did it because we were backed by the One True God and armed with both Righteousness and Guns.

If the left had their way, we'd still be a bunch of British colonies. Actually, check that, we'd probably be speaking German and goose-stepping everywhere we went. They value weakness and insist on bogging *everything* down with unnecessary nuance.

All I know is that, as a Gun-Owning Patriot, I know that I'm always going to be safe from oppression. You knock down my door, you're going to be in for a world of hurt. First, you're going to have to get through Ronald and Reagan to get to me. They may like belly rubs an awful lot, but they aren't going to let anyone endanger me or

Mrs. Tucker. But even if they get by my pups, they are going to have to come face to face with any number of firearms. My personal favorite for protection is (find a legitimate gun)

If you want to take me to a concentration camp, force me to accept homosexuality as compatible with Christianity, make me condone abortion, or raise my taxes so a bunch of lazy millennials can get paid to work on their screenplay at their local coffee shop, youre going to be disappointed. I'll never give in. To paraphrase the great Charlton Heston, if you encroach on my freedoms you'll do so after taking one of my guns from my cold, dead hands.

I see these wimps all the time ask law-abiding Gun Owners why we won't willingly limit our Constitutionally granted rights. Gee, I don't know, maybe because that puts us on a slippery slope to fascism? I usually maintain an even keel, but this is the issue that most often pushes me to my boiling point. Mainly because there are so many fools who know nothing about guns or our Constitution that insist on engaging with the experts on the topics.

I don't care that the AR-15 didn't exist when the Founders established our country. I wish it did, because we could have wrapped up the Revolutionary War a lot sooner. Because, guess what, the Founders would not only have wrapped these kinds of guns in the warm embrace of liberty, but they likely could have conceived of their existence. Yep, it's true.

It's an insulting understatement to call our Founding Fathers superheroes. They were more like super-duper heroes. They made Batman look like an avocado-toast eating hipster. Consider the greatness of these men, then consider the perfection and applicability of our Constitution to the modern world.

If they could create a document that could maintain its influence and viability in the age of the Internet when it comes to speech, or withstand the evil of radical Islamic terrorism when it comes to Religious

Freedom, do you think that they wouldn't have ensured that their ideas on guns couldn't withstand improvements to firearm technology? Oh sure, liberal, activist judges will simply gloss over these stone cold facts and spit in the face of the Constitution by calling it a "living document." When you ever read that term, please know that it roughly translates to "I hate Christian Values so I'm going to try to change the Constitution to conform better to a secular, big-government society."

I firmly believe that if George Washington, Thomas Jefferson, or any of our Founding Fathers came back to life today they would enthusiastically support our rights to own any firearm of our choosing. Heck, I bet most of them would drive with me to my local gun shop to help me pick my next gun out. And not only would they support this, but they would be aghast at the restrictions we Gun Owners face (among many, many other leftist developments in our Country).

Should I be able to buy a grenade launcher? If I desired one, yes. Do I have a practical need for one? None of your business, now please get off my porch.

In a perfect world there would be no debating this, but, unfortunately, we have all those pesky leftists muddling the issue. Because they obfuscate and mislead, it sometimes puts us gun owners in a bad light. Occasionally, I'll come across an exasperated Gun Owner who said something maybe a little too bluntly, but because liberals took offense they get to gloss over the fact that he was fundamentally right.

I've come across on more than one occasion the comment "Your dead kids don't trump my rights," in regards to radical anti-gun sentiment that inevitably crops up after school shootings. I cringe at the bluntness, particularly when it's directed at folks who are directly suffering from the tragic effects of these incidents. But... the logic is airtight.

School shootings are regrettable, but, as I've touched on, they are most obviously the result of removing Christ from the halls of our schools. When we let Satan run free what do we expect? Add in the fact that liberals have spent years vilifying guns and making it harder for good guys with firearms to enter public areas and we are basically begging for these tragedies to happen.

Ironically, even though I get angriest during these gun debates, I find myself feeling sorriest for the opposition. Often, I'm not engaging with a godless bleeding heart but with a well-intentioned yet misguided person who thinks you should blame the instrument instead of its user. I don't want these tragedies to happen, but we need to bring God back, support mental health (that doesn't mean tax me and address it with pointless government spending), and make sure we empower responsible Gun Owners to lead the charge against such senseless violence.

Every American worth his or her salt is a member of the National Rifle Association. When I discover that a new friend or acquaintance isn't registered, I'm only given the slightest consolation: I'll know exactly what to get them as a gift come Christmastime. But the NRA is a group that upholds the Values of our Great Founders.

They don't get bogged down in emotion and illogical arguments, they simply put their heads down, roll up their sleeves, and go to work defending Our most precious Constitutional Rights.

Because the NRA is so good at what it does and because their mission is quintessentially Patriotic, of course those on the left have problems with the group. Every time some nut job decides to light up a school or a department store, the godless left tells me and every other card-carrying member of the NRA that we have blood on our hands. It's the epitome of foolishness and passing the buck.

The NRA has no other agenda other than advancing the cause of preserving our Freedoms. It's not that I'm happy that the mentally unstable are able to kill others. But, what makes our Nation so amazing is that *anyone*, even the mentally insane, is endowed by his Creator to own any firearm that he chooses. It's a shame that liberals would rather sit on their parents' couch and protest on the Twitter about getting free money from hard-working taxpayers instead of going out, respecting themselves by paying their way to an education, and creating a new generation of self-respecting workers, including mental-health specialists who could help these troubled folks who feel compelled to use firearms for the wrong reasons. It's just so simple, but, I guess when you're forced to choose between leaving mommy and daddy and earning a living for yourself or being a lazy good-for-nothing and vilifying innocent, inanimate guns it's easier to opt for the latter.

Predictably, leftists don't simply direct their ire at guns and Constitution-Loving Patriots who use them, but also the gun manufacturers. It allows them to do two of their favorite things at once: Undermine the Constitution and attack our Country's most successful job creators. If I had a dollar for every time I encountered a liberal crying about the NRA lobbying for gun manufacturers, I'd probably be able to have enough money for the next decade's worth of gas for our RV when Mrs. Tucker and I go on our summer road trip.

Heaven forbid that the NRA, which is a group dedicated to preserving the Rights of Americans to own firearms, support the manufacturers that design and produce these Constitutional tools. It's a socialist's dream. They get to lie about the dangers of guns and attack the hard-working folks who have built themselves up by supplying Patriots with firearms and, in turn, have created countless jobs for the next generation pursuing the American Dream. *Please, Big Brother, take away my most effective means of defending myself and my family and go ahead and penalize those who work hard to produce them in the confines of capitalism while you're at it.* It sickens me.

I implore you, once you finish this book, do a few things: Make sure you're a licensed gun owner, join (and support) the NRA, and don't fall for the crocodile tears next time there is a public shooting. The Constitution is under siege. Our Freedoms are dangling by a thread and if we lose guns we lose the soul of the United States.

CHAPTER EIGHT: RACE RELATIONS

I'm going to say something that might seem pretty radical - if you only get your news from the mainstream media. We don't have a problem with race in this country. Well, we have a tiny problem, but it's not the kind of racism that you've been indoctrinated by our education system to believe exists.

Our country elected Barack Hussein Obama. The decision was a stain on our history in a political sense, and it validated and emboldened an army of self-entitled snowflakes to attack Patriots who love their country, but it, at the very least, demonstrated that the so-called racism that exists in our country is a hoax. We put a black man in the White House, for crying outloud, and not just any black man, but one who is likely a Muslim and very possibly wasn't even born in this country.

We have a bit of a racism problem in this country, but it's not the one that leftists think. In the past few decades, but especially in the last ten years, Whites have been vilified, held down, and blamed for all of society's ills. You can thank Barack Hussein Obama for that development.

Obama hastened the need for the Tea Party, for which I proudly attended numerous rallies. From the moment he casually sauntered out on the inauguration dais and delivered his vision for America, I was among the countless Patriots who felt anxious about the fate of our Country. I pride myself on being particularly well-read, and I was well-versed in the works of one of our Nation's most brilliant political minds, Dinesh D'Souza.

Oh, quick sidebar for you leftists: D'Souza is a brown man. He's also a political genius. Am I still racist, or are browns and blacks only OK if they fall in line with a liberal agenda that has actually subjugated them for centuries?

Anyway, D'Souza has made it abundantly clear that Obama hates our Country. He was indoctrinated by his Kenyan father to hate the Whtie man and chosen to infiltrate Our government to destroy America from the inside. He pledges to love this Great Nation but, in reality, he seeks to destroy everything it stands for and establish a godless, secular society: a liberal's paradise.

Obama was just too casual in his approach to the presidency, fundamentally disrespecting the sacred Office with his hip-hop approach to leadership. What kind of president has time to go on ESPN and fill out not one, but TWO NCAA brackets each year? (That's right, lest we anger the feminists he had to fill out a ladies' bracket.) His Correspondents Dinners made a mockery of many of our country's institutions and became little more than a roast hosted by the President of the United States to slum it with godless Hollywood sodomite comedy writers and entertainers.

Obama hated everything about our Country. He hated guns, so he vilified them. He resented that we had the greatest healthcare system in the world, so he gutted it and destroyed it. He hated our armed forces and police officers and blamed them for his perceptions of Our Country's weaknesses. He also hated the Patriots who live in the Heartland.

That's why the Tea Party became so necessary so quickly during his time in office. The Silent Majority had a moral obligation to act upon their anxiety - be it economic or Patriotic - with that man in power. People tried to blame it on racism, which was, of course, absurd. When you've got a president who is fine with running up our debt, undermining our institutions, and setting us on the path for godless socialism then race has nothing to do with it. Snowflakes whined about some of the imagery at our rallies. Well, I'll tell you what, I'm fine with depicting *any* president who hates Our Country in a hangman's noose, no matter the color. The fact that this president happened to be black was irrelevant, but the fact that you had a problem with it on the basis of skin color says a lot about YOUR issues with race.

By virtually any metric, Whites are the most positive contributors to our society. We've accomplished the most in virtually every strata. Politically, our most effective and famous politicians have been White. In business, most of the wealthiest folks are White. Even spiritually, because, in spite of the fact that my Lord and Savior Jesus Christ was born in the Middle East there is scientific evidence to suggest that he had a lighter complexion and hair color than any of his fellow citizens. I'm not saying that Whites are better or that we are inherently more capable than folks of color, but I'm just rejecting that notion that Whites are so awful, evil, and worthless when we have been the most productive contributors to where our society is today.

That is NOT the same as saying that blacks, browns, or Asians are inferior. I'm not a racist. I believe that any person, regardless of their ethnic background can find

Christ, buy into Real American Values, and live a Patriotic life to the fullest. That's were the liberals lose me and probably lose you too. It doesn't fit into their agenda when I profess my faith in my fellow men and women of color. They also don't like it with free-thinking blacks reject the shackles of liberalism (which is modern-day slavery, if you want ot be frank) and embrace the Conservative tenets on which Our Nation got its start.

I'm not a racist. I'm not a divider. That's why I proudly display an All Lives Matter sticker on the back window of my truck. We're supposed to enter the kingdom of Heaven with the mind of a child. With race, it's as simple as listening to the words of "Jesus Loves the Little Children." He loves them, regardless of color, so long as they follow His example.

Leftists love to claim that they aren't racist, that folks like you and me are the actual racists, then support groups like Black Lives Matter. I love ALL lives, you seem to only care about BLACK lives, yet I'm the one who is racist? This is a terrorist group of black supremacists and misguided White liberals who have been brainwashed to think that practicing reverse-racism is a valid way to fight for social justice.

Also, let's examine Black Lives Matter. Whose lives do they really care about? When some thug breaks the law, doesn't listen to police, and loses his life because of his illegal behavior then they want to riot in the streets. But when gangbangers in the inner-city kill other blacks we don't hear a peep. They should change their name to Criminal Black Lives Matter.

On the handful of occasions where I have had to interact with a BLM (or, CBLM) member, they usually have no comeback to quoting black-on-black crime statistics other than RACIST! I seem to care more about a larger number of black lives, but I'm the racist. Oh sure, they'll say things like *Do you ever worry about black-on-black crime unless you're defending a black death at the hands of the police?* When I inform them that I volunteer at city homeless shelters on multiple occasions and often donate food to soup kitchens in the ghetto they are either speechless or they lose their minds in anger. Apparently a white man who volunteers his time to help the blacks doesn't fit into their argument about who the real racists are.

The bottom line is that these thugs and animals, who aren't always just blacks, hate our society, hate personal responsibility, and want to blame everyone else for their station in life. It's The Man's fault that they never valued their education, decided they would rather wear Air Jordans and baggy pants than dress respectably and find a good job, and chose a lazy, lawless life where they blame Whites for their problems. Slavery was reprehensible, but last I checked I don't own slaves. None of my friends and family do either. Matter of fact, NO ONE in the United States of America owns slaves anymore. You've had centuries to get your lives in order, the statute of limitations on blaming responsible Americans for your crummy lot in life has run out.

There are some blacks that recognize this fact. I've always been pretty impressed with Dr. Ben Carson. Same goes for Sheriff David Clarke. These are black men who realize that it's OK to dress respectably and speak articulately. They aren't "selling out" or "acting white," they are just bettering themselves, recognizing that the Democrat Party hates black and brown people and using hand-out policies to keep them down, and seeing the light of Patriotism.

Are these men held up as strong black influences? Of course not. Apparently Black Lives Matter only includes SOME black lives. Meanwhile, I'm racist for believing ALL Lives Matter? Give me a break.

The criminal element that runs BLM has found a home among modern liberals and leftists because they share a common goal: destroying society as we know it. They want to defund the police, creating a lawless wasteland where criminals, socialists, and heathens can do as they please. Because they know deep down how absurd and sinful this idea is, they have to trump up charges of "police brutality," which usually amounts to examples of criminals and thugs either breaking the law or emotionally abusing police officers while skirting the line of lawlessness.

I've had a handful of run-ins with the police. In my younger (and not so younger, to be honest) days, I had a bit of a lead foot. It wasn't uncommon for me to speed a bit. I'm not proud of it, but the fact of the matter is that I've been pulled over for exceeding the speed limit on a few occasions. Now, when this happened, what did I do? Did I start screaming and carrying on about Black Lives Matter while verbally abusing these officers of the law? Of course not. I patiently waited on the officer, apologized for my excessive speed, notified him that I have a permit for a firearm, and then retrieve my license and registration. Want to know how many times I've experienced police brutality? Zero. But sure, keep telling me how evil our police officers are.

I don't doubt that there are a few bad apples in the mix. I'm not unreasonable. I just have a hard time condemning

99.9999999999999% of our brave men and women of law enforcement on account of a handful of bad actors while condoning legions of thugs and leftists activists inciting violence, starting riots, and destroying public and private property. According to the left, this makes me intolerant. Well, if believing in the rule of law makes me intolerant then so be it.

I don't applaud violence - I'm not a leftist - and I take no glee when officers justifiably use force to subdue threats. Liberals act like folks like you and me celebrate the deaths of blacks like George Floyd. Not true. It's sad that he clung to a life of criminality to the bitter end and I wish he could have calmed down before extra force was necessary, if only to have more time to get right with God. But I'm not going to pretend that the officers who were protecting and serving in this and other instances were evil or that we should make a saint out of a person who led an unsavory life and had to pay the consequences.

The fact of the matter is that far too many blacks and leftists confuse the condemnation of lawlessness with racism. That they confuse the two says a heck of a lot more about them than it does you and me. But we do not have a pervasive issue with race in this country. Every single man and woman who is born in this country has the exact same opportunity, a level playing field of freedom and equality. If you lead a principled, Conservative lifestyle as the Founders intended and follow the narrow path that Jesus Christ laid out, you will thrive. If you live as a criminal and blame the White Man for all of your problems, well, you're probably going to stay stuck in a rut.

CHAPTER NINE: IMMIGRATION

There is perhaps no better example of their lust for a lawless, globalist, secularist society than the liberals' stance on immigration. It boggles the mind that these leftists just want to let any and all persons in Our Country, regardless of how much criminal element comes along for the ride. It's a strong indication that the Democrat Party and their left-wing cronies in the media want to destroy the America you and I know and love along with everything for which it stands.

They appeal to the emotionally weak in their argumentation, yet another strong example of their illogical rhetoric. *So*, they'll ask, *these folks have been here for years, been solid contributors to their community, grown a family, and established roots, we just need to break them up and deport them?* Is that even really a question? My goodness, how far have we strayed from our center of morality.

If the foundation of any argument is criminal behavior, you can lose the extraneous detail. Did they enter the country illegally? If the answer is yes, then we don't need to know anything else. I don't care how long they've been here, what circumstances they escaped, and what they've done when they got here. If they are willing to break the law to get here then they can't be trusted to follow the law while they stay.

Lady Liberty proudly accepts the huddled masses yearning to be free. I'm a firm believer and supporter of this idea. But liberals want to distort the meaning. It's not accepting people who think that they are better than the huddled masses and think that it's OK to bypass Lady Liberty's established immigration policies.

Anyone who wants to take part in this American Experience should be given the opportunity to do so - if they go about it the right way. I'm not heartless. Yes, families should be split from their anchor babies if they broke the law to enter the country. But I think they should still be given the chance to apply for immigration the right way and, in a few years' time when they make it through the process, be able to reunite with their family. But Freedom doesn't have time for lawless warm and fuzzies.

You either apply for immigration the right way or you get the heck out of our country. It's as simple as that, no need to muddle things. This is where a strong faith in God can help you see things clearly where godless liberals see a complex issue.

God has a plan for all of us. I thank Him every day for putting me in the good ol' U.S. of A. If He wanted someone to be born here, they would be born here. If He wanted them to move to America, He would have them go about it the legal way. When leftists wax poetically about these awful hellscapes that some of these illegal immigrants are moving away from, they can't see the forest for the trees. Maybe if these people embraced Christ on such a big enough scale, they would overcome whatever oppression they may be facing in their godless societies and they wouldn't even need to move in the first place. But, since liberals removed God from schools and public places, of course they would remove him from the immigration debate. So we have a moral argument with folks who have no moral compass, that is, Jesus Christ.

So instead of crying crocodile tears for children who get to go on an extended camping trip with their friends and cousins while they wait for the irresponsible adults who had to be taken away and processed for illegal entry, pray. Instead of blaming America and those who wish to preserve Our Country's security when a child loses his life in the process of sneaking in here, pray. Maybe ask why a parent would put their child in such a threatening position, but be sure to pray too.

If more folks followed the narrow path of Christ we would lessen the need for others to escape plight and move to our country. And those who still wished to come would be more enlightened and respectful of our policies and process. So, pray, follow Christ, respect Our Country, and trust that this immigration nonsense will be sorted out with sanity ruling the day.

CHAPTER TEN: VOTING AND THE ELECTORAL COLLEGE

There are few privileges greater than the right to vote in a Free Society. When I get out of bed, the first thing I do is land on my knees and among my prayers is a sincere thank you for living in the Greatest Country in the world. Being able to vote is a big component of Our Greatness. So is the Electoral College. So, it should come as no surprise that the Democrat Party and leftists hate the way we do things.

Everyone deserves the right to vote. In theory, we and the liberals actually agree. But, Constitution-loving Patriots with Conservative Principles are ready to do whatever it takes to vote. Leftists and their lazy, selfish contingent of criminals and heathens want to make voting as easy as pulling out a phone and pressing some buttons. Our Founders literally died for our right to vote. If we have to drive a little bit out of our way or wait in line for a few minutes I think that is the least we can do.

I get so tired of hearing about voter oppression. Every time I vote, I'm in and out in ten minutes. The mainstream media tries to rationalize the laziness and lacking discipline of the average liberal voter by perpetuating the "voter oppression" hoax. Oppression? Give me a break. On Election Day, I'm up and at 'em at 5:30 so I can eat a quick breakfast and hit my polling place right as the doors open. I usually sleep in a tad later in my retirement, but I bypass the snooze button when it's Voting Day.

We only have five polling places in my entire county and we do just fine, thank you very much. Some cities have five, six, even seven polling places - for ONE city - and they complain that it isn't enough. Here's an idea, turn off the Nintendo or the TV, get a good night's sleep, and respect the practice of voting by wake up in a timely fashion and get your behind to a polling place early. I have no sympathy for folks who can't meet such a simple obligation. *I have to work, I don't have a car, I've been standing in line for three hours.* Blah, blah, BLAH.

I'd gladly WALK to my polling place and stand in line for three hours or more in order to vote. But, here come the leftists, forever the crusaders for the lazy and irresponsible. We are expected to change our way of life and make a task as simple as voting even easier and more convenient. If they had their way, folks would be cashing their welfare checks, picking up some reefer, and voting at home while they get high. Makes me furious.

That's also what makes the Electoral College so darned important. It was another example of our Founding Fathers either predicting or putting contingencies in place for the efforts of godless leftists. Not only do they want to make it so that any good-for-nothing loser with no job, no personal responsibility, and no understanding of how our society should function can just vote from home, but they want to weight things so that their votes count for more than Heartland Patriots.

Why on earth would we want to ditch a voting system that makes sure that all 50 states in our Great Union are represented come election time? I'm originally from North Dakota. If they went by popular vote and turned Our Country's elections into American Idol then so many votes wouldn't matter. Many of us in the Heartland would be dwarfed by the coastal elites. If anyone should have more influence it's us. After all, we seek to preserve the principles of this Nation, they seek to destroy them.

After President Trump soundly defeated Hillary Clinton, liberals railed against the process yet again. *She won by three million votes!* They claimed. Well, when you remove the number of illegal votes cast, account for the Russian support of her campaign, *and* factor in the damage the Obama Administration caused on the Trump campaign with their illegal spying you're probably looking at four-to-five million votes of inflation, easy.

But, come with me to fantasy land for a moment and pretend that she legitimately defeated Our President in the popular vote. Would it be fair to Patriots across the country when so many citizens live on the coasts and are seduced and subconsciously controlled by urban, liberal agendas to vote? I love democracy, but I'm not sure I want to live in a country where we just let every single person vote across the country and let the chips fall where they may.

If these liberals, who are so heavily concentrated in a few states, wanted to make a change, they could open their minds, move throughout the country, and go to places where their vote has more impact. Of course, if they were open to leaving the cocoon of leftist oppression they probably wouldn't be voting for the Democrat Party in the first place, which makes it all moot. So, instead, keep the Electoral College.

Rather than whining about the system, play by the rules. If your message doesn't play in the Heartland among REAL Americans, then maybe you need a new message. I'm a proud Republican but I don't have my head in the sand. I'd be delighted to see the creation of a legitimate, moral alternative party, one that had a few different ideas but still respected the Founding Principles of Our Country. I'm not going to hold my breath on the Democrat Party making such a change. So I'll keep voting Red, keeping respecting the process of voting, and keep supporting the Electoral College. After all, it is the Founder's safeguard against falling into a lawless, secularist society.

CHAPTER ELEVEN: STAYING INFORMED

I'm often asked how I am able to stay informed about so many topics. I chuckle at the question. I'm a pretty modest guy, so being put on the spot to address an area in which I excel makes me a little uncomfortable. But I'm also amused that so many folks, who are good people who love Our Country, don't realize that it's easy to sift through all the nonsense. Yes, there are a lot of media outlets, TV channels, podcasts, radio shows, and Internet sites out there. But the vast majority of it can be dismissed as fake news. I do have a primer for those looking to educate themselves and become a member of an informed citizenry dedicated to preserving

Our Nation. These are the outlets I utilize for information:

The Bible

There is not a single problem that you will encounter in your day-to-day life that can't be solved by studying the Good Book. That includes trying to sort things out in our crazy world. Satan has corrupted and perverted the Internet with his wicked ways, but he hasn't been able to purge it completely of God's Brilliance. Yet, anyway. So while I would encourage you to develop an intimate knowledge of the Bible, the well-intentioned but Biblically inexperienced can seek guidance for which chapters and verses to seek when tackling an issue.

Take President Trump. All of those godless liberals seek to sabotage his agenda and tear him down. If they could take the time to pull their heads out of their behinds and read Romans, they would realize that their disrespect isn't just unpatriotic, but downright blasphemous. Romans 13 tells us that we should respect those in authority because God puts folks in authority. Those liberals spent so much time worshipping a weak, corrupt president in Barack Hussein Obama that they conditioned themselves to hate strong, Christ-like leadership when it came in the form of Donald J. Trump.

But it's not just matters of respecting our greatest leaders. It can guide you to formulate theologically sound opinions on social issues, economic issues, and moral issues. Pro-Baby Killing abortion supporters pride themselves on exposing the "hypocrisy" of the Pro-Life movement. Maybe if they read the Bible they would know that if criminals are deemed worthy by society to be put to death then God wants nothing more than their execution. Don't be fooled by leftist who wish to conflate dispensing justice to thugs and druggies with the vicious murder of sweet, cuddly babies.

Liberals love to twist the true meaning of the Bible to throw it in the faces of Christians. But misrepresenting scripture and using it as a weapon is the lowest of the low.

A popular claim among the godless is that Jesus was a socialist. Nothing gets my blood boiling quicker than that. Yes, He had long hair, but He wasn't an irresponsible hippie. It was simply the reality of the grooming situation in the era in which He walked on this earth. That's about the extent of his similarities to the socialists.

Jesus Christ was a capitalist. *The* capitalist. When he said to take care of the least of these, do you think he had welfare checks for thugs and single mothers to use for nail jobs, drugs, and brand new iPhones in mind? Or, do you think he dreamed of a perfect system in which the most hard-working folks attain wealth and create opportunities for like-minded people to work their way up the ladder? The government didn't multiply the fishes and loaves for the masses, HE did, and He was gracious enough to let that miraculous surplus of food trickle down to those who needed it.

The most obvious Biblical benefits, however, come with moral issues. I can read the Bible and know that men need to lead the family and society, the homosexuals are unnatural and sinful, and that we don't need to add nuance to right and wrong. Some things are black and white. You can't condone evil, sinful behaviors in the name of "love" and "acceptance" and magically make things that fly in the face of God's Word acceptable. He literally wrote every single line of the Bible, and we have access to it's untainted power. It should be the first thing we consult each and every day.

Cable News (but be careful)

Cable news is like the Internet. In theory, it's perfect. Access to knowledge and reporting 24 hours a day, seven days a week. But, like the Internet, it has been corrupted by the godless, so you have to be discriminating in what you watch.

The best way to curate your cable news is to start with the channels you should avoid at all costs. First and foremost, MSNBC. MSNBC viewers lead hollow, godless existences. They consume nothing but hateful misinformation designed to divide and destroy our country by undermining our Conservative Principles. Luckily, based on their ratings, it seems as though it's a bunch of leftist losers preaching to a choir of leftist losers. Still, avoid it at all costs.

CNN isn't much better than MSNBC at this point. There was a time that you could still count on them to handle breaking news adequately. But since around the time of our liberation of Iraq, they have gone full-on nutjob. Everything is designed to attack conservatives. It began to rut during President George W. Bush's time in office, but it has completely gone off the rails in the age of President Trump. Apparently, all you need to do is slap a Breaking News announcement on each story, find a way to make it about a Trump shortcoming you invented, and you can call yourself The Most Trusted Name in News.

FOX News was the gold standard for years, but even it has lost a bit of its shine. I blame the loss of Roger Ailes, a real man's man and a defender of the truth and the

Conservative way of life. Money corrupts, and at Fox it turned seemingly decent women into gold-digging feminists, hellbent on committing character assassination on the man who gave them an opportunity.

There is still plenty of greatness at Fox. Sean Hannity continues to be a marvel, somehow creating one of the most intelligent, well-researched daily radio shows *and* hosting one of the best cable-news shows, perhaps *the* best, ever. Oh, and he somehow finds time to become an elite kick-boxer in the middle of all of that work. He's a Patriot with a tireless work ethic who has had to work overtime fending off the deranged assaults against our president over the last few years. I'm not big on telling fellas that I love them. It's an emotion that should exist for the most part as an unspoken truth when it comes to fathers, brothers, sons, or friends. But when I think about how much Hannity has sacrificed in the name of upholding Truth in such a godless age, well, I can't but think 'I love that man.' He's an admirable gentleman.

Tucker Carlson isn't right too far behind him. He strikes me as a smidge more intellectual than Hannity, which usually rubs me the wrong way since liberals always act like superior intelligence, education, and intellect automatically makes someway an "expert" or "more qualified" on a given subject. But he makes up for that with his evisceration of leftist doofuses. He pulls no punches. He's a master debater. I love how he'll lull a guest with a blank, emotionless stare and then go into attack dog mode. He's can't miss.

Laura Ingraham rounds at the trio of tireless Patriots that are keeping Fox relevant in the age of Trump. She tolerates absolutely no nonsense. She calls it like she sees it and it irritates liberals who exaggerate issues so they can feign outrage and throw a full-on snowflake tantrum. Take her defense of President Trump's necessary immigration policy that undid years of Obama's dangerous, laissez-faire attitude toward the millions of illegals and criminals just pouring into our country. Leftists decried the "awful conditions" of the children whose parents abandoned them when they made the decision to unlawfully enter our country and required their arrest and deportation. Ingraham has a way of crystalizing what you're thinking. When I saw footage of those kids "in cages," as the radical left-wing crazies called it, I thought 'That kind of looks like fun.' I turn on her show *that* night and she noted that it seemed like summer camp. It was as if she read my mind and formulated my thoughts more clearly and succinctly than I could. That's the kind of intelligent news coverage you must consume.

But, despite their abundance of talent, even outside of Hannity, Carlson, Ingraham - Jesse Watters and Greg Gutfeld are ten times funnier than any liberal Hollywood "comedian" you'll see - Fox has slipped a bit. They finally got rid of Shepard Smith, thank goodness. I never really liked the guy, always got a bit of a creepy vibe from him, even before he lost his mind and used those prestigious Fox airwaves to spread unhinged liberal rants about President Trump. It came as no surprise when he came out as a proud fornicator shortly after he began his crusade against Our President. It should come as no surprise that he now works for NBC.

Fox still has a bit of leftist stink in the ranks. Chris Wallace's fall wasn't quite so precipitous as Shepard Smith's, but even he has allowed the popular secular sentiment against President Trump to distort his journalistic integrity. He hasn't gone full-on liberal (yet), but he seems to like it when leftists appreciate his unfair assaults on Donald Trump's character. More or less, you're safe if you avoid any attempts at "news" on Fox, which is unfortunate but necessary.

Your best bet for straight news coverage is One America News Network. They are like Fox News on steroids, and it is a thing of beauty. When I tune into a press briefing I can spot questions from an OANN, I can spot one of their reporters from a mile away. Though don't pretend to humor the godless left with gotcha questions masquerading as hard-hitting reporting. They are Conservatives and Patriots first and journalists second, which is sort of ironic since they have become, by far, the best, most trusted, most informative source of news in the United States of America.

Podcasts

My son turned me onto podcasts a couple of years ago and it has been the most positive development in my life since I retired. He finds the ones I like, pushes some buttons on my phone, and they show up every time a new episode is released. I've mentioned my fondness for Buck Sexton, and his podcast is very good. You can also catch up on Conservative radio heroes like Hannity or Rush Limbaugh in podcast form. But, the best in the business is a young man by the name of Ben Shapiro.

I will say upfront, he has yet to accept Jesus Christ as his Lord and Savior. I have added Shapiro to my nightly prayers in hopes that he will see the light and turn from the flawed spiritual path he has chosen. That said, he is a proud supporter of Israel and one of the most brilliant minds that I have ever encountered anywhere.

Liberals like to refer to their heathen demigods as "intellectuals," because they coat their godless beliefs in a veneer of elitist academia. It makes them feel better about themselves and the flawed opinions they have developed. Not Shapiro. The beauty of him is that when you catch bits and pieces of him, you'd never have an idea that he was as intelligent as he is. But he is prolific and his intellectual pursuits span far and wide. I've seen him *eviscerate* a pro-abortion activist and have time to put on a film-reviewer hat and expose a feminist agenda in those Star Wars films in the span of one day. I applaud his tireless commitment to defending Conservative Principles. Now, let's just pray he finds Christ and gets Baptized so such a brilliant soul isn't denied entry into God's Kingdom.

Radio

Being a Patriot in this day and age can be demoralizing. We are inundated with lies and manipulations everywhere we turn. The media is a liberal machine hellbent on indoctrinating our children with leftist propaganda. AM radio, however, offers a bit of a Conservative oasis in the desert of leftwing nonsense.

You've got Hannity. Dennis Miller, who marries cutting-edge comedy with no-nonsense political opinion. Mark Levin, a long-time Conservative voice who I see a lot of in Ben Shapiro, from his *destruction* of liberals to his smooth, soothing voice. All of these folks are great at way they do, but make no mistake, Rush Limbaugh is the king.

Limbaugh put Conservative Radio on the map. He blazed the trail for so many, wading into the cesspool of godlessness to create a beacon for Real Americans who didn't realize how sorely they needed three hours of good old-fashioned Conservative Values coming out of their radio speakers each day. I can count on my hand the number of times I've missed his show in the last thirty years. Since my son got me set up with the podcasts I have more flexibility to listen when it's most convenient. But it will be a sad, sad day for Our Country when Rush signs off for the final time. It is a credit to the leadership and integrity of Our President that he honored this wonderful man with the Presidential Medal of Freedom. If ever there was a person deserving of this honor, it's Rush Hudson Limbaugh.

Books

We are blessed that so many of the greatest minds in Conservative Media are so prolific in what they do. How selfless is it that Sean Hannity, Laura Ingraham, Mark Levin, and so many others have time to broadcast their views on television, radio, and books. It reminds me of President Trump, who took a paycut to take office and do his best to lift us out of the eight-year rut we suffered through as a country. Most of these Conservative voices are millionaires many times over and don't need to work through so many avenues to enlighten us. It is appreciated though.

Your best bet is to stick with these renaissance men and women. In the Trump Era, so many conservative voices have lost their way. I used to greatly admire George Will. He was a strong, unflinching Conservative voice. Now he suffers from Trump Derangement Syndrome.

A good rule of thumb is to avoid books from self-proclaimed Conservatives who slum it with left-wing media outlets, such as newspapers. Stick with the unapologetic Conservatives from Fox, the good folks at OANN, or tried-and-true Patriots like Donald Trump, Jr. You don't need to muddle your worldview with unnecessary, extraneous nonsense. Find a few voices you can trust and lock onto them with all you've got.

Documentaries

Documentaries can be dangerous. They are like public education. In theory, they perform a service for the greater good and the advancement of knowledge. In reality, they have been hijacked by left-wing activists who wish to advance their agenda by indoctrinating folks in the name of "education."

But, just as you can find a trusted, faith-based home-school curriculum, you can find documentaries that don't entertain liberal nonsense and lies. There is one name that stand out above the rest. If you are committed to preserving Our Nation and you haven't checked out the work of Dinesh D'Souza, then you aren't doing your part.

D'Souza exposes the lies of the left each and every time he releases a documentary. He revealed that Obama's presidency was the culmination of his year's long plot to seek revenge on his White, colonialist oppressors. He outed Hillary Clinton as perhaps the most corrupt person to ever seek Our Nation's highest office. His documentaries should be required viewing for everyone in America. The world would be a much better place.

If you're an otherwise uninformed person who knows that Conservatives fight to uphold Our Nation's Founding Principles who wants to become a more active civic participant, but you feel overwhelmed by where to start, fear not. You shouldn't feel compelled to consume the volume of Conservative Media as those of us who devote each day to solidifying their understanding of how Our Country should run. My list isn't a syllabus of everything you need to use right now, it's merely a guide for the cream of the Conservative crop as you wade ever deeper into the pool of knowledge, righteousness, and Patriotism.

Our country is in a scary place right now. We become more divided by the day. It's sad, but what's sadder is that there doesn't seem to be a light at the end of the tunnel.

The problem in America is extremism. Extremists can corrupt fundamentally sound and moral stances. So imagine what they can do when they latch onto flawed, dangerous ideas.

CLOSING THOUGHTS

It is my hope that this book awakened something in you. There is only so much hate and misinformation that a person can take before they have to open their eyes and see reality. My dream scenario is that each and every person who reads this book will have a moment of clarity on how to formulate their opinions, perceive facts, and ground themselves in reality.

www.ingramcontent.com/pod-product-compliance
Lightning Source LLC
LaVergne TN
LVHW091108150826
845673LV00002B/744

* 9 7 9 8 6 6 7 4 6 7 0 7 6 *